Life...
it goes Better with Laughter

21

SHORT STORIES ABOUT LIFE'S FUNNY MOMENTS

ANDY ALI

ROCIMA PUBLISHING
Trinidad and Tobago

Rocima Publishing
22 1/4 EMR Valencia
Trinidad and Tobago
www.rocimapublishing.com
info@rocimapublishing.com

ISBN: 978-976-96063-8-8

Cover illustration by Bryan Jordan (2017)

Published and printed by Rocima Publishing

Trinidad and Tobago

Contents

Indulge me for a few moments while I tell you about a dream that I consider a significant one. In this dream, I saw myself standing at the entrance of my workplace and as I entered, there was a big banquet where a long buffet table was situated. I saw the familiar faces of my coworkers and they told me to take a plate and help myself on the buffet table. So I did.

As I proceeded down the buffet table, I noticed something strange on it. It was a slab of a very big snake on a platter. I put my plate down and did not partake of anything. After I placed my plate down on the table, I was suddenly transported outside of the building where I saw an even bigger snake with an emotionless face and a brown-spotted body coming to my direction from behind some trees. It was the biggest snake that I have ever seen—even larger than the snake from the movie *Anaconda*. It moved with lightning speed as well. It maneuvered around me and passed with a great force that shook me where I stood. It then headed toward the building I was from.

Then I was suddenly transported to another place that reminded me of St. Mark's Square, Venice. As I stood in the middle of this Square, I felt freedom that I have never felt before. It felt like I could do or become anything I ever wanted and it wouldn't be difficult—a freedom that I could feel and was so real. Then I woke up.

On the 6th of August 2016, my wife Stacy had taken our children—Anastazia (Ana, for short) and Zane—to Mayaro Beach, to spend time with family and friends. I stayed at home to work on something I can't even recall to this day. My children were excited to spend time with their cousins and just enjoy the beach.

On the next day at around 10:00 a.m., I received a call from Stacy where she told me that our nine-year-old daughter, Ana, drowned. It's the call no parent would want to receive. I fell to my knees in shock. I just couldn't believe what Stacy was telling me over the phone. I have to say that Stacy was an extremely strong woman because she had to deal with trying to revive our daughter on the beach. It turned out my father-in-law, Morris, drowned as well. So, Stacy lost her father and daughter on the same day. I lost the apple of my eye and as I was kneeling on the floor, I asked God for mercy, grace and strength to go through the rest of the day. God knows our family needed it, and still do.

So what does this have to do with my dream? I had it about two years before Ana passed away. I shared it with a trusted friend and she explained to me that the dead snake on the platter was my daughter's life force that had gone out and the familiar faces of my coworkers represent my colleagues who supported me and stood with my family during our time of bereavement. The large snake I saw outside the building represented a power I received to stand during the time of my daughter's passing. When the large snake did not devour me, it was like I received a power that enabled me to stand. The rest of the dream represents a positive outcome of true freedom despite how things may seem.

During one of our discussions, Stacy told me that she's not afraid of dying since Ana passed and neither am I. The fear of death has been removed somehow, as well as the need to judge any person or situation, after this experience.

This book would not have been written if not for the encouragement of one of my dearest friends. His name is Aaron Gayah and he put the thought of writing this book in my head. However, this wasn't the first time I was told about writing a book. My late aunt, Molly Lima, was a spiritually inclined woman and she once prayed with me and told me that I would be a person writing books. I almost forgot about what she said until Aaron challenged me to write this book.

I would also like to thank my wife, Stacy Sammy, who's simply a tower of strength, my son, Zane Ali, my very heart, Maureen Ali-Harangee, the best mom, Aldwin Harangee, Doris Jageshar, the best grandmother, Natalie Cameron, Anthony Cameron, Kinda Sandy, Ronnie Roberts, Summer Sandy, Zurina Bolvin, Lisa Bolvin, Wendy Neves, Brent Neves, Taran Ramoutar, Donna Ramoutar, Robert Sammy, Eleanor Sammy, Judy Stephen, Celine Stephen, Rex Brazil, Ravi Mungalsingh, Margaret Lee Chee, Dixie-Ann Creese-Lee, Carlene Voisin, Daryl Ramnarace, Nora Ramnarace, Winston Ali, Sean Ali, Farouk Ali, Debbie Ali, Sheila Ovid, Mary Moore, Shelly-Ann Edwards, Yukmai Marsang, Soroya Volney, Anuradha Ramdath, Anisah Ramautarsingh, Michael Roopchan, Sunita Jagat, Candice Gaines-Ramjohn, Gobin Sookram, Rossi Sealy, Nicholas Beharrylal, Earlin Stanford, Gerrard Sampson, Jason Chattergoon, Nadia Gajadhar, Andrea Stewart, Moonilal Lalchan, Himalaya Boodoosingh, Imtiaz Easahak, Dawn Hackett, Shanti Maharaj, Naveen Sharma, Winston Lochan, Abiola Alphonso, Khari Denoon, Amanda Hunte-Balgobin, Roshan Jaggernauth, Hardy Hobson, Dawn Seusankar, Elizabeth Sookermany, Joel Brooker, Joel Fraser, Sharon Pirali, Cassiann Ramdhan, Roshni Bhowansingh, Tameeka Luces Lima, Christopher Mathura, Waheeda Rahim, Karen Bonyun, Charmaine Coutou, Lisa-Marie Springer, Nicole Kempo, Sharda Jankiepersad, Debra Soomai, Kamal Ramnath, Elizabeth Richardson, Stephen Mc Shine, Vindra Ramnanansingh, Dharamraj Harry, Jenny Narinesingh, Lisa Goodridge, Chris Sookram, Julia Thompson-Romano, Jacqueline Martinez, Ghenet Simonette, Selwyn Trimm, Steve Nakhid, Alister Sampson, Terry Ragbir, Dave Ali, Sunill Seelal, Ronald Roberts, Derek Basdeo, Stacy Basdeo, Damien Harry, Tricia James-Roberts, Darryl Roberts, Ronald Payne, Devon Telesford, Allan St. Clair, Mervin Lookhoor, Salim Mohammed, Nigel Ali, Pravin Bissessarsingh, Leslie Dowe, Sufya Shaheed, Lebrado Maloney, Reagan Seepersad, Levi Dick, Safraz Khan, Major Sarwan

Boodram, Sensei Steven Jimerfield and David Tam who made the writing of this book possible.

All of the stories you will read in this book are true and the majority of them are from personal experiences. Some of the stories were given to me by friends and family, and the names of the characters have been changed to protect the identities of the persons who willingly contributed their stories in the hope of a good laugh.

I dedicate this book to the memory of my daughter who always wore the brightest smile and found the good in every situation. Thanks for reading and God bless!

Foreword

Because teachers and students spend a major part of the day together, they impact each other on many levels, both positively as well as negatively. Making a difference is often viewed as the role of the teacher, but at times the student's personality is so powerful that roles can be reversed in profound ways where the student leaves the lasting impression. Ana's presence had that ability: to make you sit up, pay attention, take note, enrich you and leave you spellbound all at the same time. Her classroom signature was keeping anyone who would listen enveloped in the story she had to tell which she told in grand style, impressive, as if it were a performance that we all attended; perfect in every way. Ana's charisma and impeccable speech kept you interested and made all that she had to say seem like the performance of a lifetime, forever to be etched in your minds. There was never a topic that she did not have a riveting story to supply. For her young age her repertoire of experience was fascinating. Dearest Ana, the beautiful smile, the flick of your hair, the swing in your step—you have blessed our lives and enriched us as no one else could.

Dixie-Ann Creese-Lee
Teacher 1
St. Gabriel's Girls' R. C. School
Republic of Trinidad and Tobago

1

School Days:

THE LUNCH-STEALING BULLY

I believe most people would agree with me when I say school days were the best days of life. You didn't have a care in the world and all your meals were provided by your parents. They even gave you money to spend. I enjoyed my school days but they were filled with challenges. Sitting still and reading were difficult for me, especially for an extended period. However, I buckled down and did what had to be done.

There was one incident that stands out in my mind as one of the most hilarious events in my secondary school days. That was the day the lunch-stealing bully got back his due for taking our food. This was in an all-boys Catholic school so there was lots of testosterone in the atmosphere. To add some flavor to this story, I will dub the lunch-stealing bully with a title. Let's call him "Lunch-stealing Larry."

Lunch-stealing Larry was one of the most miserable and mischievous characters you would ever meet. He would always start a fight with smaller students and steal their lunches afterwards.

One awesome and glorious day, Lunch-stealing Larry stole lunch from one of our classmates. This classmate was Larry's regular victim but on that particular day, he was absolutely frustrated and fed up of Larry's constant abuse. So, a few of the other boys, headed by one of our fearless classmates, whose code name was "Chinee," devised a plan to get back at Lunch-stealing Larry. Chinee informed the entire class of his plan to take partially dried dog poop from the school yard and place it in Lunch-stealing Larry's bag so when he sticks his hand in his bag, he would get dog poop all over it. Everyone agreed that the day of justice had arrived.

The plan took action and the dog poop was acquired and carried into class with military precision and placed into Lunch-stealing Larry's book bag. The class waited for Lunch-stealing Larry to arrive and venture into his bag. It was the classic calm before the storm as everyone snickered to themselves with anticipation of what would take place.

As Lunch-stealing Larry entered the classroom, everyone carried on as normal but the tension in the room was bursting at the seams. You could just feel that something was up and it was going to be ridiculous. Suddenly, Larry unzipped his bag and everyone softly sighed as he placed his hand into his bag, pulled it out, and said, "What the mother…"

The entire class erupted with laughter. Those who were standing stooped. Those who were sitting rolled on the floor. Others ran out of the classroom due to uncontrollable laughter.

However, the climax moment of that entire event was when Lunch-stealing Larry looked at his hand. He could not believe it was dog poop, and smelled his hand just to make sure. After this, he became enraged and went around trying to intimidate people asking, "Who put poop in my bag? Who put poop in my bag? You put poop in my bag?" Most students just laughed at him. He was consumed by shame that his eyes were filled up with tears and the spirit of the bully was broken that day. The news of what happened to Lunch-stealing Larry spread throughout the school. Of course, Larry reported it to the principal but no one squealed.

One thing I learned from watching the event unfold is that life is truly cyclic. What you sow is what you reap. Lunch-stealing Larry's misdeeds came back at him like a ton of bricks and there was nothing he could do about it except waddle in shame. Thankfully, in time, his behavior improved for the better. It's a miracle that he turned out to be a productive member of society.

A Day at the Office:
This Meeting Is Off to a Good Start

It was approaching 4:00 p.m. and the weekly meeting was drawing near. I couldn't recall the name of the young lady who organized the meeting so I entered the meeting room in my usual cavalier attitude and most of the usual suspects were in attendance. At that moment I exclaimed, "What's the name of the skinny girl with the big boobies again?"

As faith would have it, she emerged from under the board-
room table where she was attempting to connect the desktop
computer to the projector. The entire room exploded with laughter including the young lady whom I described, bordering on ob-
jectification. It was truly a funny moment and my timing could not
be more perfect. I must say she took it well and said, "It's okay,
Stanley," after I apologized profusely.

All I can say is that life has a funny way of reminding you that
the person you're talking about may be in the room and everyone
may know it except you. Do you know what else was funny about
that moment? When I saw her emerge from under the table,
I remembered her name. I probably should have waited a few
moments more.

◆ 3 ◆

An Adventurous Young Couple:
PARKING, IF YOU KNOW WHAT I MEAN

I'm twenty-two and live with my mom at her two-story house. My mom stays upstairs and I stay downstairs. I would usually wait until my mom goes upstairs to sleep so I could invite my friends to come and "buss ah lime" or hang out.

One evening, while my mom and I were watching the news channel, I stepped out to pick up my girlfriend. I assumed by the time I return home, my mom would have been upstairs, sound asleep. However, when I returned home with my girlfriend, we noticed the TV room door was open and the television was still on, so my girlfriend and I tiptoed out and backed out the driveway as quietly as possible while trying our best to control our laughter.

We drove for a while and came upon a quiet location at the beach. As nature would have it when two young people are alone

together, they really want to join together. As things heated up in the car, along came some visitors from the local police station. One of the officers began tapping at the window and shining his flashlight into the vehicle.

"Come outside now!" the policeman exclaimed. "Don't bother to put on your clothes. Just come outside."

"We'll first put on our clothes and then go outside," I simply told my girlfriend, Well, you could imagine how embarrassed we were. One of the police officers started speaking to me with a big grin on his face.

"Young man, your face looks familiar. Are you Barry's brother?" he asked.

"Yes, I am," I responded in a calm and soft tone, To prevent further ridicule to my girlfriend and myself, I preempted the police officer's next words by interjecting, "I would like to make a contribution to the police officer's year-end Christmas party. Could you tell me where I can make my contribution?"

"Of course," the officer exclaimed. "Right here!"

Talk about the power of a proper inducement in a time of need. My girlfriend and I were allowed to leave with our dignity intact and a memory of an event that will bring us laughter when we reminisce on our younger days. Safe to say we laughed all the way home like two adrenaline-seeking junkies, who barely escaped a life-and-death situation.

Remember, if you're ever caught in a similar situation, put on your clothes first!

4

My Boss:

THE ONLY GIRL IN THE 'BOYS' CLUB

As a boy, I always loved movies and I found the silver screen and television captivating, even mesmerizing. So, I went to a Winter Intensive Acting Program at The Lee Strasberg Theatre and Film Institute in New York. It was a fabulous experience and not to mention my first winter that I celebrated in fine style wearing sweaters, coats, and scarves like a true New Yorker.

In one of our classes at the institute, our lecturer, Mr. Zurkowski, said something that stuck with me. He said, "In acting, you have to find the comedy in the script . . ."

I liken this to life where there are so many funny moments. You may not recognize them now but in retrospect, you may find them totally hilarious.

One of my first jobs was to be an assistant to a lawyer of a highly successful and important organization that contributed greatly to the economy. She was no ordinary lawyer. This person was highly respected and had a professional reputation that extended globally. In simple terms, she was one of the best in her field.

She needed an additional assistant and I needed a job. I had applied for an administrative assistant position at the company where she worked and I received a call from their Human Resources representative that they would like to interview me. So, I arrived at the office and was ushered in to see my future boss. Her first words to me were, "When we saw your resume and you were the only boy who could type, we wanted to meet you."

Needless to say, I got the job.

My boss had her own style of communication. For example, she would hardly use the desk phone to call me since my cubicle was just outside of her office. She would simple exclaim, "William! Come for a moment."

If I wasn't at my desk, it progressed to her stepping out of her office and into the corridor, asking, "Where's William? Did

you see William?" Then she would proceed a little further down the corridor and shout to the next person she sees, "If you see William over there, tell him I'm looking for him!"

This was the routine if I wasn't at my desk. Sometimes if I was in the washroom, I would hear her calling me and if another coworker was in the washroom, they would say to me in a comedic tone, "Hey, William! Your mother looking for you."

This was usually followed by laughter.

Despite that, I admired my boss's command of the English language. She had a gift of writing efficiently. She would peruse an entire page of text and with her magic red pen, break it down into a paragraph and it would mean the same thing. Of course, this made me feel illiterate on more than one occasion. She would often tell me, "Doing law is very boring. The bulk of it is lots of reading."

I enjoyed looking at the way she conducted herself during board meetings, as she was usually surrounded by all those male legal representatives from other companies. She always conducted herself with confidence, professionalism, and a sense of humor. She never took herself too seriously.

What I admired most about her was her straightforwardness. If she liked you, you would know. If she didn't like you, you would know that too. I believe that's why we always got along.

5

THE VAGRANT ON THE CORNER

I often wonder how some people end up homeless or desti-tute. Each person is different and possesses a unique perspective about life and the challenges that may come their way. You hear all kinds of stories about people making unwise choices from drug abuse, alcoholism, uncontrolled rage, and bitterness. I remember listening to a prominent speaker and this person said, "Most mental issues stem from unforgiveness . . . ." If that is true, then it would certainly explain the behavior of the vagrant on the corner.

I often observe this particular vagrant because he sits on the corner opposite the school my daughter goes to. Sometimes, he would sit there quietly minding his own business but at other times, he would be most vocal. He would face the wall with a stick in his hand and express his disgust at a female person who

hurt him in the past. You should witness him in action. He has all these gestures and his facial expressions display anger and deep emotional turmoil. His actions with the stick in his hands would cause most pedestrians to cross the street to avoid being hit if he decided to launch at them.

There is nothing funny about watching someone act out in pain because of past hurt, but the comedy in this story is that my cousin reminds this vagrant of the woman who betrayed his trust. Let me explain.

My cousin, who happens to be a lawyer, works in the vicinity where the vagrant performs his rants. She is of mixed decent and looks more on the East Indian side because of her long straight hair. Apparently, whenever the vagrant sees her walking by in close proximity, he becomes enraged and begins to cuss out loud and call her all sorts of degrading titles. My cousin's reaction to this barrage of nomenclatures is to walk fast, with her head up straight and her eyes gazing slightly back just in the event that she would have to make a run for it.

Just picture a well-dressed lawyer in high heels making haste during the performance of this emotionally charged homeless person. Life certainly has its funny moments and this is definitely one of them.

◆ **6** ◆

THE CATS ARE IN THE BAG AND AIRBORNE

At this stage in my life, I have love and respect for animals. Dogs and cats are adorable and bring lots of joy to adults and children around the globe. You can't help but fall in love with them, and they are extremely faithful and loyal to their owners.

My son had a cat for his first pet and for his second pet, he had a dog. He cared for them deeply and treated them with love. However, my experience with pets when I was a boy was quite different.

When my son would lovingly play with his pets by giving them hugs and kisses, I would do the same. But after a while, I would chase them around and scare them.

I had a pet cat when I was a boy and I remember wanting to test the theory that a cat always lands on its feet. So, at the top of the staircase, I would pick the cat up and toss it in the air toward the bottom just to see if the theory was right. Of course, the poor cat didn't always land on its feet but after

several repeats, he got the hang of it. You could also imagine how difficult it became to find my pet cat when I called it.

There's something about cats that intrigued me as a boy. Maybe it was the way they meow or the high pitch of their growl and hiss when you provoke them.

There were several stray kittens in the area and while I was playing in the yard, an idea popped into my head. When I usually threw my cat in the air, it would make a loud meow. So, naturally I wondered how loud would that sound be if I threw a bunch of cats in the air.

I found a crocus bag, grabbed a piece of twine rope, started collecting the stray kittens, and placed them in the bag. I managed to get about five kittens. I proceeded to tie the mouth of the bag with the twine rope to secure the unsuspecting subjects of my experiment. I then made my way to the wall and started swinging the bag around and around. You can hear the kittens meowing together like a grand symphony. It was a sound I remember to this day.

I suddenly released the bag into the air and over the wall. The sound from the bag increased in volume as the cats landed in the neighbor's yard. To be honest, I don't remember what happened after that but my experiment was a grand success. I made the cats sing and not to mention, fly. My aunt often told me that I was a naughty boy and she was right when I look back at that event. Boys will definitely be boys.

7

READY OR NOT, HERE COMES 'MADMAN GOPIE'

I know the title of this book is: *Life...It Goes Better with Laughter,* and these stories are supposed to contain humorous topics, but I felt that I needed to include this story because it was so profound. It was the first time that I remember being truly afraid.

If there's one feeling most human beings would have experienced in their lifetime, it's fear. Most of us are afraid of something or even someone especially when we were children. Either we're afraid of the dark, our neighbor's dog, or a teacher. One way or another, fear sometimes gets the best of us. It can stop us in our tracks or make us do something superhuman like scaling a wall twice our height.

As a boy, I often spent time at my grandmother's house with my sister and cousins since my mother had to work on weekends.

I enjoyed staying there because she made the best sada roti. I just loved eating hot sada roti and butter. There's nothing like it. It was like mother's milk to me. Of course, hot sada roti and butter wouldn't be recommended by Tony Horton as part of a healthy diet but it was a regular staple in Grandma's house.

In the street where my grandmother lived, there was a mentally disturbed individual who passed through twice a day. He looked like a vagrant with only his pants on. He had a big black beard, his hair was unkempt and he carried a stick. He also wore no shoes. Everyday like clockwork, he would pass through the street once in the morning and once in the evening. While he walked, he would speak aggressively to himself and swing his stick as if he was fighting with someone. If there was one person all the children that lived on my grandmother's street were afraid of, it was that vagrant who we all called, "Madman Gopie."

Madman Gopie not only looked unstable; he was the real deal crazy. The only words that we recognized coming out of his mouth were profanity. When my cousins and I spotted Madman Gopie

coming down the street, we would all scamper and find a place to hide until he would go past our house. If you didn't hide and Madman Gopie saw you, he would pick up stones and throw them at you. We've had close calls with Gopie so nobody messed around him. When you heard his rantings coming down the street, it was time to ride out and take cover. Usually, we would run in the house or hide behind the house if we couldn't make it to the front door.

One evening, I was walking up the street from the standpipe to my grandmother's house. Just my luck, I spotted Madman Gopie coming down the street. A sudden crippling fear came over me. My heart rate rose exponentially almost to the point of palpitations, and I started breathing heavily. I said to myself, *Please don't see me! What to do? Oh God, what to do?*

It was too late for me as Madman Gopie and I locked eyes. He started to cuss loudly. I just ran like there was no tomorrow. Madman Gopie took aim with his stick and launched it behind me. I felt the impact of his stick as it struck my right arm. I didn't stop running until I reached my grandmother's house. I dived behind the couch and hid.

I don't recall feeling any pain when his stick struck me but I knew it did. I just felt extremely petrified. I didn't move from behind that couch until my aunt came in and asked what's happening. I peeked from behind the couch like a scared little rabbit afraid to come out. I couldn't even speak for a while. I was overwhelmed by fear. My aunt hugged me and urged me to calm down because she started to become anxious. My grandmother entered the living room along with my sister and cousins and I finally told them what happened.

I often wondered what happened to Madman Gopie. If most mental illnesses are caused by unforgiveness, I wondered who hurt him so deeply that he couldn't forgive.

8

SCARING COUSIN SALLY

My grandfather loved gamecock fighting. He was a gambler at heart and he actually owned a few gamecocks which he meticulously took care of. Those gamecocks would be trimmed of excess feathers so their bodies would appear streamlined and made lighter so they could maneuver well in a fight. They were well-fed and were even given multivitamins to ensure proper nutrition. My grandpa would also tie one of their legs to a balancing rope he had made to train them to gain balance while he moved the rope back and forth. This man had it down to a science.

My cousin Rob was charged with the responsibility of assisting my grandfather in taking care of his gamecocks. He would often go into the fowl coop and feed the gamecocks, and I would assist him whenever I visited. He would also prep the gamecocks for their training on the balancing rope. It was interesting to watch these gamecocks being taken care of like little children. I was jealous of these gamecocks as they would actually get massages with Bay Rum.

One day, while I was assisting Rob with his gamecock duties, his little sister, Sally, came into the fowl coop and she was prancing around like little kids do while simultaneously speaking a mile a minute. Rob and I looked at each other and it seemed like we were thinking of the same thing—we should scare Sally the hell out of the fowl coop. I picked up one of the sticks lying around and Rob picked up another stick. We looked at Sally in a menacingly manner and started speaking in a heavy tone, saying, "We're going to take you, little girl! We're going to take you and hide you away in the bush."

You could imagine little Sally's reaction. She started to scream and tears flowed down her cheeks while she exited the coop. We chased her and struck the sticks on the ground close to her feet. She screamed even louder and made her way into the house. We turned around laughing like two clowns and headed back to the fowl coop.

Suddenly, we heard our names being called out loudly. "John and Rob, come out here!" It was my aunt and she had Sally at her side. My aunt let us have it. "Look at this child, she can't even speak. You boys are terrible. Why did you scare her like that? I will beat the two of you jackasses today so help me God!"

I believe she even cussed us but I can't recall exactly because when she said "beat," we thought of running away as fast and as far as we could.

I must admit though, after seeing little Sally so distraught, I felt sorry for what we did to her. She was a sweet little girl and she didn't deserve to be treated that way. But boys being boys, the temptation to scare her was too great.

◆ **9** ◆

SUSAN TOUCHED ME

Attending primary school was lots of fun. I had a won-derful teacher and great friends. We had one thing in common and that's playing! We loved to run and hide and just have fun in school. It was a mixed school and by that, I mean both boys and girls. My classmates were quite friendly and easygoing.

I figured at that age, children don't see any differences in each other. You're a girl and I'm a boy. My name is Sam and your name is Shirley. So let's play together. Life was easy!

One day during class, I was sitting next to Susan. She was a pleasant girl, and we got along well. All of a sudden, I felt Susan's hand touch my thigh under the desk. Now, we would touch each other all the time while we played catch or tag but that time, it was different. It felt a bit strange. It was slow and steady and it had intent. Her hands moved up my thigh and very close to my special little no no place. Then her hands took my hand that was close to her body and she guided my hand under her dress very close to her special little no no place. Honestly, I had no idea what was going on but Susan obviously did. I felt nervous and I looked around to see if anyone noticed what was happening. Susan then interlocked my fingers with hers and moved closer to me. We just sat there looking at each other. Talk about strange and exciting at the same time!

I never forgot that event because it was so out of the ordinary. I never told anyone until years later and had a good laugh about it. I wonder where Susan is now.

10

My Friend's Unfriendly Sister

I had a friend in school named Niall that everyone considered to be rich. His family had their own business and he had a driver to drop him to and from school. He was a typical privileged child but he was also friendly. At least friendlier than his elder sister who attended a prestigious all-girls college. She was a total snob.

Niall was gracious and would have some of the boys over to his home where we would play and eat hot dogs and burgers. It was good fun. His sister, however, never mingled and always appeared to have a serious demeanor. Whenever she spoke, it sounded condescending somehow, like you were less but you couldn't figure out why.

After school was over, I usually walked home or sometimes took a taxi if I had enough money left from my snack allowance.

I was raised in a single-parent home because my father passed away when I was very young. My mom usually worked late and she taught us how to travel using taxis and maxi taxis. As I got older, I appreciated her efforts to make us self-reliant. Being a single mom is not the easiest job in the world but she did what she had to do to provide for her children.

One evening after school, Niall offered me a lift home as it was on his route home. I gladly accepted. We ended up playing after school was over and the time ran away from us because his driver came late to pick him up. We both hopped into the vehicle and we were off. Niall's sister was in the vehicle too with a con-descending look on her face while I was smiling from ear to ear because I didn't have to walk home. Thank God for small miracles. I arrived home that evening and all was well.

The next week, Niall and I ended up playing again after school and it was late so he offered me a ride home. Again I accepted without hesitation. We excitedly entered the vehicle and I was smiling from ear to ear again. This time, Niall's sister turned to me, looked at me with contempt, and said, "Why are you always coming into this vehicle? Why are you taking a ride with us so often now?"

Well, the smile I had on my face turned into a blank ex-pression and everything seemed to go quiet around me. I had the strangest feeling like I was worthless and I actually felt physically smaller. I was so embarrassed I couldn't even speak.

When we arrived at my home, I simply exited the vehicle and the driver looked at me with a bit of sympathy. It's like he felt my shame.

Needless to say, that's the

last ride I took home with Niall. He was friendly and courteous the next day even though he knew how his sister had embarrassed me. However, that event didn't stop us from playing together. We continued to be friends.

I narrated the story about Niall's sister to my wife one day as we sat on the bed while she was playing with my hair. As I told her what happened, tears began to flow down my cheeks. I couldn't believe that I was carrying the hurt from that event as an adult. Since then, I always make a conscious effort to be mindful of what I say to children especially my own.

I saw Niall's sister at a mutual friend's birthday party some years later and it turned out my wife knew her family. I mentioned to her that I thought she was a total snob and she was mean to me when I was a boy. She simply got up, went inside the house, and started to cry.

Niall's sister and I met again and I told her that I forgave her for what she said to me as a boy. She was delighted. She admitted that she really felt terrible about the entire situation. Now, we always speak whenever our paths cross, and I definitely feel lighter.

11

GRANDMA KEPT ME UP ALL NIGHT

My grandmother lived simply and was certainly a woman who knew how to make the best of whatever she had. She was able to raise five grandchildren on her pension and by all means, that was a miracle. There was always something in the house to cook as she was a regular shopper at the Sunday market. She would have her crocus-fashioned market bag while inspecting produce and looking for the best deals. I can't remember her having a wallet as she would often use her bosom to keep her money safe. Not to mention, she walked extremely slow. You could fall asleep waiting for Grandma to finish shopping.

Grandma was quite a demanding character and she certainly had moments where you would have to be patient with her. As she got older, it seemed that she became more demanding.

One night, one of her granddaughters was staying with her in her room to keep her company because earlier on she complained about not feeling well. This task of spending the night with Grandma turned out to be an extremely trying experience for my cousin, Abi.

It turned out that almost every half hour, Grandma would get up and call out to Abi asking, "Abi! Are you there, girl? Abi! Are you there, girl?" Abi would jump out of bed thinking something was wrong and she would respond with bated breath, "Are you okay, Grandma? Are you okay?"

However, Grandma was just fine as she was just ensuring that Abi didn't leave the room. If there was ever a case of separation anxiety, hands down to Grandma who had the symptoms.

After they settled down, Grandma was at it again.

"Abi! Abi! I'm feeling thirsty. Can you get me some water, please?"

"Sure, Grandma. I'll get you some water." Abi, replied, still half asleep.

There's something you may have realized in your interactions with older people. They sometimes put on a helpless voice as if they are seeking sympathy. Grandma was a master at that. I truly believe it was an effort on her part to make you feel sorry for her somehow.

Going back to my story: Abi returned to the room with the water and Grandma had her refreshing drink. Then, they both settled back down. Moments later, Grandma called out again,

"Abi! Abi! I want to use the washroom."

As I mentioned before, Grandma walks extremely slow. So, you can just imagine how long it took Abi to assist Grandma from getting off the bed to actually making it to the washroom and all the way back to the bedroom. Not to mention Abi had to work the next day so she didn't get much sleep at all.

Abi and Grandma returned to bed after going to the washroom and settled in.

"Abi! Abi! Are you there?" Abi was already feeling the effects of her lack of sleep.

"Yes, Grandma! What is it this time?" Abi answered in a rough tone.

"Abi, don't be angry with me. You sound like you're angry."

"No, Grandma. I'm not angry. What do you need?"

"Nothing," Grandma answered. "I just wanted to make sure you're there."

Always remember, if you want to get a good night's sleep, don't sleep next to your grandmother. Oh, did I mention, Grandma also snores.

12

I Had Too Much Curry Duck, But It Tasted So Good

Every country has its unique food that is synonymous with the culture of the people. For instance, when we think of Italy, we think of pizza, spaghetti, gelato, and tiramisu. The Republic of Trinidad and Tobago has its favorites as well. We have crab and callaloo, crab and dumplings, doubles, roti, bake and shark, and of course, curry duck. The food in Trinidad is tasty, not to mention that this country is the home of the scorpion pepper. I believe that pepper has a mean of over 1.2 million Scoville Heat Units. It's hot.

Without a doubt, one of my personal favorites is curry duck. It's quite a treat and you could have it with basmati rice and dhal, with roti, or you can enjoy it on its own. Either way, it tastes really good.

One of the best curry ducks I have ever tasted was cooked over an outside fireside. That by far was the most delectable. So, you could imagine how much I ate. I even brought home a con-

tainer full of it and ate it over the next two days. I was in curry duck heaven. I savored every bit of that curry duck for those two days. I even sucked and chewed up the bone to draw out every ounce of flavor that I could possibly get. It was blissful.

The next morning, I suddenly woke up with a growl in my stomach. I felt the urge to make my way to the toilet as fast as I could. You guessed it! That curry duck came out with a vengeance and it didn't want to stop. Every time I thought my bowel movement had stopped, it started again. I couldn't exercise the courtesy flush fast enough and the airflow through the window seemed to be taking its time. All my discharges were messy and had the makings of an extreme case of diarrhea. The odor seem to take over the atmosphere much like a chemical asphyxiant. It was so bad that I actually lost consciousness until my wife came in and woke me up.

"What happened to you, boy? You passed out," she asked jokingly. You could imagine her nonstop laughter. She actually covered me with a towel while I lay on the floor trying to regain consciousness. Soon after my daughter walked in.

"What's wrong with Dad? Is he sick? And what's that smell?" she asked.

"Your father passed out. He ate too much of that curry duck," my wife replied with laughter. Well, those two had a good laugh while I was lying on the floor.

I eventually got up and cleaned myself. I could still hear the laughter of those two coming from the next room. It was an experience I'll never forget, and knowing my wife and daughter, they wouldn't let me forget it either.

All in all, the curry duck really did taste good, but sometimes too much of a good thing is just too much.

13

WILL I EVER GET A GOOD NIGHT'S SLEEP AGAIN?

I clearly remember the day my daughter, Ana, was born. It was a Wednesday, on the 4th of July 2007. It was a glorious day and it's amazing that she was born on the same day that Independence Day is celebrated in the United States.

She was a special child. She came out of Stacy's belly with her mouth wide open, letting out a loud cry.

"She's a singer and she looks big," Stacy said.

"She's a bawler!" the doctor replied. He then placed Ana next to Stacy. My wife kissed our little girl. Of course, I was filming the entire thing but moments like those you don't even need a camera to remind you.

We took the little pumpkin home and we soon discovered that her rhythm for sleeping was different.

During pregnancy, Stacy would feel Ana strongly kicking during the night. That kept Stacy awake. In the morning, Stacy would be tired and her eyes usually looked puffy because of her lack of

sleep. This pattern of waking during the night and sleeping during the day continued after Ana was born and it wreaked havoc on us as parents. We were worn.

Imagine being up till 2:00 a.m. trying to put this child to sleep. We took turns to ease each other but it still took its toll. I can't remember reaching to work on time for almost six months or more. We would employ singing, storytelling, walking, rocking, listening to Hillsong music and dancing to get this bright-eyed, bushy-tailed child to sleep. Once I was even tempted to place her in a cupboard and close the door because her crying just overwhelmed me. Thoughts of throwing her out the window entered my mind. Thank God for Stacy who came to the rescue.

All I can say is that it truly takes two to tango, especially when raising children. This is a serious business and we as parents have to be committed to taking all the challenges. We also have to remember to laugh because we sometimes felt that we would have been stuck at that stage forever.

14

OH NO! NOT ANOTHER NAPPY CHANGE!

I must say that I love children. They bring joy to my life in incomparable ways and I just can't imagine my life without them. They grow up so fast that it seemed like a dream and I had to pinch myself to be convinced that this was really happening. One moment they are babies cuddling in your arms and the next moment, they are calling you Daddy and telling you they want to go to KFC to eat chicken and fries. I feel like a stationary observer in Einstein's theory of relativity—time dilation, to be more exact.

One task that stands out to me when my daughter Ana was a baby was the constant changing of diapers. It's like this child wouldn't stop having a bowel movement. I would hug and kiss her and all of a sudden, I would get a whiff of something and I knew it was time to change that nappy again. Sometimes, I would hide because I figured out that she needed her diaper changed and I just couldn't muster the strength to do it anymore. My wife would call out to me but I would be quiet. I soon discovered being quiet didn't help much because that would prompt her to look for me. When she found me, she would state how tired she was and ask me to change Ana's nappy again. How could I refuse the woman who bore my children when she asks in such a polite manner? So, I was at it again—changing one thousand diapers and counting.

One thing I observed when I was changing Ana's diaper was how trusting she was that this person, her father, would gently clean her little bottom. She would laugh and move her hands up and down as if she was excited for me to do it. At times, I had to hold my breath because the odor was a bit overwhelming. I would say to her, "What did you eat, child? Boiled eggs and sausages? You little stinky bottom."

Afterwards, changing her nappy didn't seem that bad. I forgot about the negative thoughts I had toward this diaper changing event and got caught up in her beautiful smile and rosy cheeks. I started kissing her and tossing her up in the air which made her laugh even more. She was truly a little bundle of joy.

15

GRANDMA, PLEASE DON'T BE NAKED

As I look back at my childhood days, I can't imagine them without my grandmother. Grandparents are so wonderful because they actually spoil you and this upsets your parents to say the least. You were allowed to do all the things that your parents could not have gotten away with because your grandparents always had your back. I'm sure this may not be true for all grandparents but it was like that for me. My grandmother spoiled me as best as she could. I always got extra food which would explain my chubby state as a boy. I didn't mind one bit as eating was one my favorite hobbies.

When you become an adult, life takes you in different directions. I spent a lot of time finishing up school on weekends while working during week. The opportunities to visit my grandmother grew less and less but I would take the time to visit whenever I could.

We had a good family friend named Shri who took the time to

check on Grandma to ensure she was fine during the course of the day. Shri would usually call Grandma before visiting her.

One day, Shri called Grandma's number but there was no answer. He tried several times but Grandma didn't pick up the telephone. Naturally, Shri became worried so he hurried over to Grandma's house. He looked through the glass door into the living room but he saw no one. Shri dialed the number again. *Maybe Grandma decided to take a nap or probably she was in the washroom*, he thought. Shri dialed the number and the telephone in the living room started to ring. Grandma slowly walked in but Shri's head was down while the phone was ringing and he didn't see Grandma making her appearance without any clothes on. Shri then lifted his head and spotted Grandma walking past the chair next to the telephone but she didn't see him. Shri couldn't believe what he was seeing and started saying to himself, *Grandma, you're naked! Grandma, please, don't be naked! Oh no, Grandma, don't sit down! Down sit down, Grandma!*

Grandma sat down and Shri experienced the grave effects of gravity on her body. They then looked at each other but Shri quickly ran away from the front door.

"Hello, who's calling?" Grandma said as she picked up the telephone.

"It's me, Grandma. I was just calling to find out if you're okay. You weren't answering your phone when I called earlier," Shri, replied, doing his best to keep his thoughts together.

"I was in the bathroom," Grandma responded, while laughing.

"Okay, Grandma, I was just checking up on you. We'll talk tomorrow."

According to Shri, it took him a while to purge the image of naked Grandma from his mind.

You may think calling first before you visit someone would be a good thing but at times it may not be. However, I believe that in Grandma's thinking, when you reach a certain age, you don't really care who sees you naked.

16

GRANDMA'S CALLING MY PHONE BUT SHE RECENTLY PASSED AWAY

Life is truly short and sometimes, we take it for granted that people will always be there. When I received the news of my grandmother's passing, it truly saddened me, but, on the other hand, she wanted to join her husband and her best friend who passed earlier.

She was eighty years old and she has had her share of hurts. When my daughter passed away, she was truly depressed and every time she would see me, she would breakdown and start crying. She didn't even want to visit us anymore because seeing Ana's picture made her sad.

All of the family gave support during the time of my grandmother's passing. My aunt stayed with my cousin a few days in the apartment downstairs that Grandma occupied. Grandma preferred to stay there by herself. She refused to move upstairs with my cousin after her husband passed on.

Shri, our family friend, being his usually kind self would

check on my aunt who was staying at my cousin's house. Whenever my aunt came to visit my grandmother, Shri would chauffeur my aunt to and from her destination.

One day, while my aunt was still in my grandmother's apartment, she decided to call Shri so she could make arrangements with him to take her home the following day. Keep in mind that my grandmother passed away a few days ago so just imagine Shri's surprise when his mobile phone lighted up with an incoming call that read: *Grandma Calling*. Shri couldn't believe what he was seeing. He totally forgot that my aunt was staying in my grandma's apartment and it took him a while before he got his thoughts together. His mobile phone kept ringing and he just kept staring at the screen. Shri was literally paralyzed and his heart rate accelerated exponentially. He couldn't move. Thank God, he was not driving at the time. Eventually, he mustered up the courage and answered, "Grandma?"

"Shri, it's Auntie Margaret. I wanted to go home tomorrow so I'm calling to arrange with you," the voice on the other line replied. Shri breathed a sigh of relief and told Auntie Margaret that he would return her call in a few minutes. He laughed at himself as he totally forgot about Auntie Margaret. It was such an intense moment for him that he perspired profusely. Nothing like a call from the dead can scare the living daylights out of you.

17

LITERALLY, THE SHOCK OF MY LIFE

Children really need to be supervised. You always have to check on them to ensure that they're not getting into any trouble especially if the house becomes too quiet. You may have a child with a quiet personality who enjoys playing alone but you still need to keep an eye on their activities. If you and the child are in the same room, you may drop your guard a bit thinking what can go wrong since they are so close and if something does go wrong, you can react quickly. But one day, something did go wrong and my mother was in the same room with me.

I remember my mom crocheting on the bed and my sister was sitting next to her. I, on the other hand, was fiddling with our Panasonic radio, turning it on and off, looking at all the dials, and opening and closing the door for the cassette tapes. The radio was still plugged into the wall socket so it was fully powered and I was having fun investigating this object before me. I unplugged the female end of the power cord connected to the radio and began looking at it intently. Meanwhile, the male end of the power cord was still connected to the wall socket. I noticed some hairpins that my mom left lying around on the counter. I picked up one and began to wonder what would happen if I would stick this hairpin into the female end of the power cord. So, I stuck the hairpin in and I suddenly felt this excruciating pain flow through my fingers followed by a loud sparking sound. I screamed out like a banshee! I then dropped the cord, held on to my hand, and ran all the way into the gallery bawling and crying. My mother unplugged the cord from the wall socket and came out behind me with my sister following. I couldn't even speak because I was in so much pain.

"Let me see your hand, son, let me see your hand," my mother kept saying. I just kept on crying, running, jumping, and rolling on the floor because the pain was so intense.

Eventually, I settled down a bit and my mom looked at my hand. It was already swollen and the tips of my fingers looked slightly burnt. She started screaming and shouting at me for being such

an idiot. She even beat me for scaring her. She was really concerned about me and after I received my spanking, she hugged me and kept me on the bed with her so I could rest after my theatrical performance.

As I reflect on this event, I think of how caring my mother was and how much concern she had for me even though I got spanked. It was out of love.

Children do things at times without thinking of the consequences. My mother warned me several times not to play with the radio while it's plugged in but I didn't listen. I ended up hurting myself and causing her unnecessary trauma.

I'm truly sorry, Mom. Much love.

◆ **18**

Just Sharing Kicks with Tim and Waldo

I have a friend named Tim and he is what we call a real "limer" in Trinidad. He loves to hangout, knock back a few drinks and just have a good old time whenever possible. He has his own business and has experienced many ups and downs but still keeps going. He has settled down a bit as age brings wisdom but I remember a story he told me of one his friends named Waldo.

Waldo was also a business owner but a much older gentleman and he was a bit on the wild side. Tim and Waldo hadn't seen each other for a while and they crossed paths at a favorite watering hole. There they sat down and gave each other an update on life's progress.

"Tim, my friend, don't ever make the mistake and get married. It's the worst thing you could ever do in life."

"Waldo, I'm already married," Tim replied, with a big smile on his face.

"Oh nooooooooooooo!" Waldo said loudly. "Oh no, Tim! Oh, God,

no! Let me tell you something, my friend. You better listen to me. Don't ever get divorced because that's worse than marriage," Of course, Tim laughed out loud because at that point, they were both intoxicated and Waldo's advice sounded so ridiculously funny.

Apparently, Waldo went through a trying divorce and he ended up signing over most of the control of his business to his wife. It was a tough experience for him because his wife hired some "muscle" and they threatened to beat him up and break a few of his bones if he didn't sign. Waldo wasn't the best-behaved individual. His wife just had enough of his wild ways and decided to end their marriage relationship. But she wasn't going out empty handed.

The two men continued their conversation about life's highs and lows. Tim started to explain to Waldo about the latest expression he heard.

"If a young lady ever tells you that you have a serious case of

'xactly,' what do you think she means by that?" Tim asked Waldo,
Waldo pondered it for a while.

"Tim, I have no idea what that means but I'm sure it's something ridiculous."

"When someone tells you that you're suffering from a serious
case of 'xactly,' they mean that your mouth smells 'exactly' like
your bottom," Tim explained. At that, Waldo spat out his drink
and almost rolled on the floor in laughter.

Sometimes when you want to have a good laugh, there's nothing better than sitting with an old friend and just talking about
life at your favorite watering hole.

◆ **19** ◆

JOHNNY GOES DOWN AGAIN AND AGAIN

Johnny and Ryan are cousins and they have quite the reputation of being the highlight of a party. They both love to dance and their personalities are equally energetic. They were regulars at the club scene and not a weekend would go by without finding them at the most happening party. They worked hard and partied even harder. Their energy and charming personality made them a hit with the ladies as well. They would be seen tearing up the dance floor with all the lovely ladies.

Johnny suffered from syncope and at times, he's been known to pass out while dancing or during a conversation. His cousin Ryan would then come to his rescue by dragging him into a corner and leaving him there until he regains consciousness.

On one occasion, Johnny was in the middle of his energetic dance routines with a lovely young lady. It was a Spanish song so they were Latin dancing and, boy, were they on fire. They were spinning and executing all the fancy footwork and Johnny

was in his element. Suddenly, Johnny twirled his dancing partner with the intention of catching her but instead of catching her, he passed out and his dance partner hit the floor like a loaf of bread. Let me just say that this event was a crowd stopper.

Ryan, along with some of the young lady's friends, ran to the dance floor and assisted her. He then turned his attention to his cousin and dragged him off the dance floor and placed him by the corner of the bar. Without a doubt, the young lady was embarrassed but she wasn't seriously hurt. Her friends quietly ushered her out of the club while Johnny was resting on the floor.

Johnny was at it again. This time, Johnny and Ryan were having a conversation with friends at a local bar during an after-work lime. The music was playing and everyone was having a good time. There were some lovely young ladies in attendance so Johnny introduced himself to one of them. They started chatting and exchanging numbers when all of a sudden, Johnny hit the floor and the young lady screamed out like someone jumped out of nowhere and scared her. Ryan immediately ran over and quietly reassured the young lady that everything was fine and Johnny was going to be okay because this usually happens to him as he suffers from syncope. You could imagine how startled she was as this was her first time experiencing such an episode. Ryan did the usual and dragged his cousin Johnny by the corner of the bar until he regained consciousness.

One thing is for sure, after meeting these two cousins, you'll never forget them.

WHAT HAPPENED TO SPACEMAN

I spent a lot of time at my grandmother's house during my boyhood. In her neighborhood, there were other boys that my cousin and I were allowed to play with. They were fun to be with. Two brothers I clearly remember were Bryan and Dave. They had bikes and I learned to ride using their bikes. I also learned how to make slingshots and hunt doves from their guidance. They were wild and adventurous and as a boy, I liked nothing better.

Dave had a nickname. We called him "Spaceman" but I can't recall why. Their father owned a vehicle repair garage and he was really good at his job but most of the time, he was drunk. Bryan and Spaceman were also skilled with their hands—a gift they inherited from their father.

I remember Spaceman drinking as a boy so he had an early start with alcohol. He was just mimicking what his father did. However, he never tried to influence me or my cousin to drink. He treated us like we were his younger brothers and looked out for us. We lost touch with Spaceman as my cousin migrated to the United States and I moved on with life in Trinidad.

One day, I visited my grandmother and as I was approaching her front door, a man called out to me and approached me. I didn't recognize him at first until he introduced himself as Dave. I couldn't believe it. I stood there almost dumbfounded for a few seconds. He looked like a caricature of a bottle of Grand Old Parr and his breath smelt like alcohol.

"You don't remember me, Fat Man?" He asked. I was chubby as a boy so everyone in the village called me, "Fat Man."

"Spaceman?"I responded hesitantly.

"Yes boy! It's me, Spaceman!"

My reaction to him was mixed with both joy and sadness. I was happy to see him after all those years but I felt sad that he turned out to be a full-fledged alcoholic according to my grand-mother. He would regularly visit my grandmother and assist her with chores in exchange for money so he could purchase alcohol.

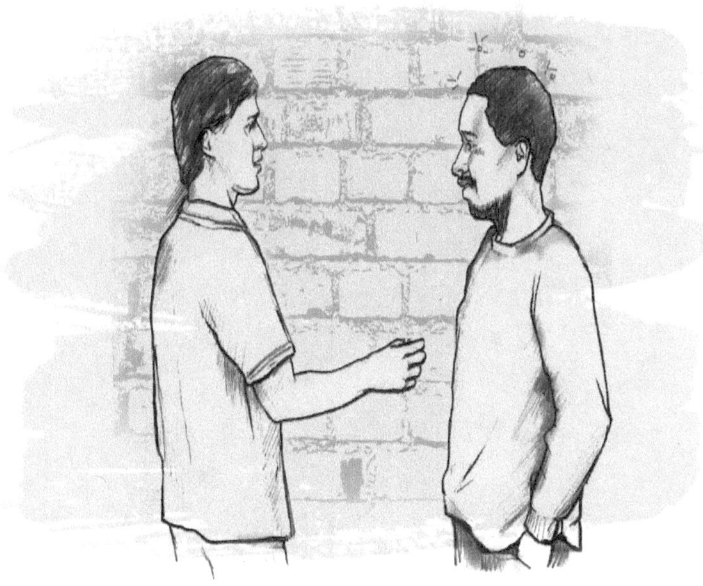

He was always intoxicated. My grandmother told me that Spaceman drinks every day and she can't recall that last time she ever
saw him sober.

My grandmother would speak to Spaceman about his alcohol
abuse but after a while, people have to take responsibility for
themselves. To date, Spaceman never did. He's still an alcoholic
and he seems to like it that way.

21

STACY AND THE HERD OF GOATS

My wife, Stacy, grew up in a household with seven siblings and they all had fun as children. Life was simpler then as she would put it. The Internet wasn't a requirement for purposeful living and children spent most of their free time playing outdoors. They would play catch, ride bikes, run, jump, skip and climb trees to eat their favorite fruit when they became hungry.

To put it holistically, they were one with their environment and it supplied their needs. All was well.

On evenings, it was common to see the goatherd making his way down the hill. His goats crowded the road as they made their way home from grazing the fields. The children would usually stop playing and observe the goats as they went by speedily, bleating in unison. Some of the goats would have the ropes around their necks as they went by. After the goats passed by, they left some droppings to indicate that they were there and you would some-times have to play hopscotch to avoid landing on the little round presents that they left on the road.

One day, Stacy, and her siblings were outside playing and en-joying the evening shade that the cloud cover provided. Suddenly, in the distance, they heard the sound of hooves making its way down the hill close to home. They stopped what they were doing and ventured closer to the road to get a better look. As the goats made their way down the hill, one of the ropes that were tied around a ram's neck became extended toward where the children were standing. It seemed to pick Stacy as it hooked unto her foot and slippers. Just imagine what took place next. That's right. Down went Stacy as she was dragged into the middle of the herd of goats while she screamed her lungs out. Nevertheless, those goats kept on moving and so did Stacy as she was liter-ally trampled by the herd and carried a few feet. Her siblings raised an alarm but it was over within twenty seconds. However, it was the longest twenty seconds of Stacy's life as she franti-cally made her way out of the middle of the herd when her foot became loose from the rope. The goats left her with a souvenir bump on her upper nose bridge.

Of course, today we can laugh at Stacy's clash with the goats but she always tells me of how helpless and afraid she felt being carried away by the herd. She was eight years old at the time and it's definitely one memorable event from her childhood.

About The Author

Andy Ali is the first-time author of *Life…It Goes Better With Laughter*, dedicated to his daughter Anastazia Mischa Ali, who passed away at the age of nine in 2016. Andy is a CMMS Support Specialist by profession and lives in the lovely twin island—the Republic of Trinidad

and Tobago. He enjoys spending time with his family, meeting new people, traveling, exploring new cuisines, eating coconut and soursop ice cream, the more than occasional KFC, and watching exciting movies such as the James Bond series, the Mission Impossible series, the Indiana Jones series, and the like. He's an avid Combat Readiness Practitioner (self-defense) and a P90x3 fan. He believes that things always seem better in the morning and once there is life, there is hope.

E-mail: sazcapstoneinv@gmail.com

My Testimony

A few days after my daughter passed away, I was at the lowest point that I have ever been in my life. I felt devastated, helpless, hollow, hopeless and for the first time in my life I really had no idea what to do. What direction should I go in? How do we move on from this as a family? What do we do? What do I do?

Everything we held dear was shattered. All our plans, hopes and dreams crashed. We were at ground zero and I literally had no strength left. I felt drained mentally, emotionally and physically. I had a big gaping hole where my heart was. I now understand how a person can take their own life because this feeling of hopelessness is real. I remember leaning against the wall in my home with my forehead and left shoulder touching the wall and as I was about to fall apart, all of a sudden, I felt a hand come around my chest and held me. There was no one in the house but me at the time. It was a right hand and it was gentle, yet strong. As the hand covered my chest, I felt the fingers extend and I fell into this hand without falling apart. It held me for a few moments as I was literally suspended by this hand and then it raised me up and straightened my posture while simultaneously giving me strength. Then I felt the hand sink into my chest and filled the space in my heart.

It took me some time before I could speak about this experience. The more I thought about what happened the more I believe I need to share it. After experiencing this miraculous event with this 'hand,' it does not mean that I miss my daughter any less but I hold on to the experience in my heart that GOD in His sovereignty, chose to come down from heaven to reassure me that my family and I are in good hands and so is my daughter.

I AM grateful to GOD for the HOPE that He gave me especially when I needed it the most.

Thank you.

Andy Ali
Republic of Trinidad and Tobago
Thursday 22nd November 2018

Recommended Reading:

Brian Tracy. 2009. Reinvention: *How to Make the Rest of Your Life the Best of Your Life*. New York. AMACOM, a division of the American Management Association.

Jack Canfield. 2015. The Success Principles(TM) - 10th Anniversary Edition: *How to Get from Where You Are to Where You Want to Be*. New York. HarperCollins Publishers.

Wallace D. Wattles. 2007. *The Science of Getting Rich*. New York. Tarcher-Perigee.

Stormie Omartian. 2001. *The Power of a Praying Husband*. Oregon. Harvest House Publishers.

Major Sarwan Boodram. Second Edition 2018. *Personal Safety, Self-Defence Awareness & Assault Prevention*. Republic of Trinidad and Tobago. Safari Publications Co. Ltd. E-mail: pumasociety2013@yahoo.com.

Major Sarwan Boodram. First Edition 2017. *Survival Tactics*. Republic of Trinidad and Tobago. Safari Publications Co. Ltd. E-mail: pumasociety2013@yahoo.com.

Sensei Steven Jimerfield. 1999. *One-On-One Control: Safe Street Tactics for Law Enforcement*. Ray and Roo Enterprises.

Sensei Steven Jimerfield. 2001. *Cold Weather One-On-One Control*. Ray and Roo Enterprises.

Judith R. Bernstein, Ph.D. 1997. *When the Bough Breaks: Forever After the Death of a Son or Daughter*. Kansas City, Missouri. Andrews McMeel Publishing.

Levi Lusko. 2015. *Through the Eyes of a Lion: Facing Impossible Pain, Finding Incredible Power*. Nashville, Tennessee. W Publishing Group, an imprint of Thomas Nelson.

Robert P. Redenbach. 2007. *Self Defence in 30 Seconds!* Queensland. Courtney Ballantyne Publishing.